Coding With
Roblox
For Kids

An unofficial Guide to Mastering Roblox Scripting and Building Games using Lua Programming.

Uchenna Ihekaire

Printed in the United States of America

© 2024

Printed in the

USA

Copyrights

All rights reserved. No part of this publication may be reproduced, stored in a retraval system or transmitted in any form or by any means, electronic, mechanical, photocopying, recording, and scanning without permission in writing by the author.

Printed in the United States of America

TABLE OF CONTENT

INTRODUCTION 1
    WHAT IS ROBLOX? 1
    ROBLOX SETUP 2
    LET'S PLAY ROBLOX ON YOUR MAC! 5

GETTING STARTED WITH ROBLOX 7
    WHAT IS ROBLOX AND WHY IS IT AWESOME? 7
    LET'S EXPLORE ROBLOX STUDIO! 8
    INTRODUCTION TO THE ROBLOX STUDIO INTERFACE 9
    YOUR FIRST SCRIPT: HELLO, ROBLOX! 11

EMBRACING VARIABLES 13
    UNDERSTANDING VARIABLES 13
    ASSIGNING VALUES 16
    ASSIGNING VALUES TO MULTIPLE VARIABLES 17
    CREATING AND USING VARIABLES 19
    EXERCISE: CREATING A COUNTDOWN TIMER: 21

BRINGING WORLDS TO LIFE WITH INSTANCES 23
    INTRODUCING INSTANCES: OBJECTS IN YOUR GAME 23
    INTEGRATING WITH MODULE SCRIPTS 32
    WHAT ABOUT INHERITANCE 33

LOOPING ADVENTURES 39
    LOOPING THROUGH INSTANCES 43
    EXAMPLE: ANIMATED OBSTACLE COURSE 45

MAKING CHOICES WITH CONDITIONAL STATEMENTS 51
    INTRODUCTION TO MAGIC CHOICES IN ROBLOX 51
    CREATING GAME INTERACTIONS WITH "IF-ELSE" STATEMENTS 53

ORGANIZING AND SIMPLIFYING WITH METHODS 58
    INTRODUCTION TO METHODS: ORGANIZING YOUR CODE 58
    CRAFTING YOUR PERSONALIZED SPELLS! 61
    USING METHODS FOR EFFICIENT CODING 61
    EXAMPLE: CREATING A CUSTOM AVATAR 62

MASTERING TABLES FOR DATA MANAGEMENT 64

Understanding Tables: Organizing Data 64
What are Tables? 65
Creating and Modifying Tables 66
Using Tables for Inventories and Scores 67
Example: Building a Leaderboard 69
Challenge: Designing a Virtual Pet Game 70

YOUR ROBLOX SCRIPTING JOURNEY 72

What You've Learned 72
A Look Back: The Magic You've Unleashed 73
Inspiring Creativity and Continuing Your Adventure 75
Why Keep Going on Your Quest? 75
More Adventures Await! 76
A Challenge to Ignite Your Spark! 76
In Conclusion 77

GLOSSARY OF ROBLOX SCRIPTING TERMS 78

GLOSSARY 82

INTRODUCTION

What is Roblox?

Have you ever heard of Roblox? It's a super awesome game that lets you have a ton of fun while also learning how to do something cool called coding. Coding is like using a secret language to make your very own games and stories!

In Roblox, you get to play all sorts of games like "*Work in Pizza Place*" or "Shark Attack," and guess what? While you're playing, you're learning how to code too! But that's not all! If you have a game idea that's been bouncing around in your head, you can bring it to life using something called Roblox Studio. You get to design your very own games and let your imagination run wild!

Now, you might be asking yourself, "Why should I learn coding on Roblox?" Well, here are some really good reasons:

- Roblox uses a special language called Lua, and it's easy and fun to learn.
- Playing on Roblox is like being on a playground, but you also get to learn how to code at the same time!
- Lots of kids just like you are playing Roblox and having a blast.
- You can even create your very own games and share them with all your friends.
- Plus, playing these coding games can make you feel super confident and proud of yourself and your awesome skills!

But wait a minute, you might be wondering, "*Is Roblox safe?*" Absolutely! Roblox games are made especially for awesome kids like you, and they're designed to be super safe and tons of fun. Your parents also have tools to help them choose the best games for you, and there are experts who make sure everything stays safe and totally awesome.

So, how can you get started with coding on Roblox? Well, it's quite simple:

- First, open up Roblox Studio.
- Then, have a blast creating your very own characters and cool places.
- Don't worry if it feels a little tricky at first. Just like any awesome game, it takes a bit of time to learn.
- Roblox Studio has everything you need, and the best part is, it's all free!
- Keep practicing and before you know it, you'll become a total Roblox coding superstar!

Get ready to jump into the amazing world of Roblox and let your creativity shine! Put on your creativity hat and let's have a blast while we learn how to code together!

Roblox Setup

Are you excited to start having a blast on Roblox? Just follow these steps to get started:

- First, open up a web browser like Edge, Firefox, or Chrome.
- Type in the Roblox website address and press Enter.
- Once you're on the Roblox website, look for a game that catches your interest and click on the big green Play button.
- Sometimes, you might see a message that says Roblox is getting ready to play. Don't worry, just give it a moment to load.
- Once it's ready, Roblox will open up right in your browser.
- Now, go back to the Roblox website and choose a game that you want to play.
- Click on the "*Play*" button.

Sometimes, you might see another message asking if you want to use Roblox. Just click on Roblox and then click OK. If you check the box that says "remember," you won't see this message again next time.

And that's it! Now you're all set to have a fantastic time playing and staying safe on Roblox!

Setting Up Roblox Studio

Hey there, my awesome friend! Are you super excited to start creating your games? Let's get Roblox Studio all set up together!

First, let's make sure your computer is ready for all the fun:

- If you have a Windows computer, you'll need Windows 7 or a newer version (if you have Windows 10, there might be some extra stuff you need, but don't worry about it for now).
- If you have a Mac computer, make sure it's running macOS 10.13 or above.
- Make sure you have at least 10GB of free space on your computer.
- Your internet speed should be pretty quick, as fast as you can run!

Now, let's install Roblox Studio. It's super-duper easy! Just follow these steps:

- Open up your web browser and go to roblox.com/create.
- Click on the "*Start Creating*" button, and a window will pop up.
- Find the "*Download Studio*" button and give it a click.
- Look for a file called RobloxStudio and open it. The process might be a bit different depending on whether you have a Windows or Mac computer.
- Once it's open, click on "Launch Studio" and sign in with your Roblox account. If you don't have one yet, no worries, you can create a new account.

- Hooray! You're all set up and ready to dive in!

First Steps in Coding on Roblox

Coding on Roblox is like doing incredible magic tricks! You'll use a super cool language called Lua. Here's a fun thing you can try to get started:

- Open Roblox Studio and start a brand new game.
- Add a platform to your game and give it an awesome name like "DisappearingPlatform."
- Make sure the platform is nice and big for you to jump on.
- Anchor the platform so it stays put and doesn't fall down.
- Now, it's time to add some code that will make the platform vanish when you step on it! This part might be a little bit tricky, but trust me, it's totally worth it when you figure it out.
- Have an amazing time exploring Roblox and let your creativity shine like a superstar!

Keep Safe with Roblox Parental Controls

Roblox is an incredibly awesome game, and it wants to make sure that everyone stays safe while having a blast. Here's how parents can lend a helping hand:

Parents, follow these steps to ensure your kids' safety on Roblox:

- Go to the Roblox website and log in.
- Click on the gear icon at the top.
- Choose "security settings."
- Turn on "Account Restrictions." This way, you can keep an eye on the games your kids are playing.

There's also an "Interactions" button to keep online chats safe and fun. Remember, it's always great to know who your real friends are!

Why Roblox is SUPER AWESOME!

Playing Roblox isn't just loads of fun; it's also fantastic for your brain! Here's why:

- It ignites your imagination and lets it soar high!
- You learn really cool computer skills that will be super useful in the future.
- It's a fun way to dive into coding and discover its magic.
- You become a superstar problem-solver!
- Trust me, you'll absolutely love learning even more while playing Roblox!

Let's Play Roblox on Your Mac!

If you have a Mac computer, here's how you can play Roblox:

- Use the Firefox browser to go to the Roblox website.
- Once you're on Roblox and logged in, find a game that looks super fun and click on the big green Play button!
- A little box will pop up, telling you that Roblox is getting ready on your computer.

It's time to start the game!

There's a little box that asks if you always want to use Roblox to play. Click on it, so you don't have to do this every time. Then, click on "Choose," and a Finder window will show up.

- Open the Finder window. It's where you look for files on your Mac.
- Press three keys together: CMD, SHIFT, and G. This will open a special box where you can type something in.
- In that box, type the following address: /Applications/Roblox.app/Contents/MacOS/Roblox.app

- Press the RETURN key, just like saying "Go!"
- Now, you'll see Roblox.app. Click on it, and then click "Open."
- A new box will pop up. Look for Roblox.app in that box and click "Open Link."
- Yay! ☐ Roblox should start. Next time, you can simply click the play button to jump into your favorite Roblox games!

Installing Roblox Studio

Hey there, future game designer! Are you ready to unleash your creativity and build your very own Roblox world? Let's get Roblox Studio set up on your computer for some awesome fun!

- Begin the Adventure: First, go to the Roblox website and log into your amazing account.
- Search for the Magic Button: Once you're in, find one of your own awesome games and look for a button in the top-right corner. It might look a little different, but you'll recognize it. Click on it and choose "Edit."
- Magic Happening Alert: Get ready for the magic! A message will pop up, letting you know that Roblox Studio is setting up its magical tools just for you.
- Open the Door to Creativity: Once everything is ready, Roblox Studio will open up all by itself! Ta-da! You're now equipped to start creating incredible worlds.

Get ready to have a blast and let your imagination soar as you embark on your Roblox Studio adventure!

GETTING STARTED WITH ROBLOX

What is ROBLOX and Why is it Awesome?

Imagine a world where you can be anything you want! You could be a brave knight saving a kingdom or a master chef running a busy restaurant. Welcome to Roblox, a really awesome place where you can do more than just play games—it's like a whole galaxy of adventures made by people just like you!

Roblox isn't like your usual game—it's a canvas waiting for you to create and bring your dreams to life. Every game on Roblox was made by someone with an idea. Maybe it's racing dragons, exploring space, or just hanging out in a virtual café. There are so many things you can do!

But why is Roblox so cool?

- *Let Your Imagination Go Wild*: It's like having an endless toy box. You can build, play, and show off your creations to everyone!
- *Everyone's Invited:* Whether you're playing on a computer, tablet, or phone, Roblox is there. And with millions of players, you'll always find someone to join your adventure.
- *Learn While Having Fun:* When you play Roblox, you're not just having a good time—you're also learning cool stuff like coding and game design!

See, Roblox isn't just a game—it's a world where your dreams can come true.

Let's Explore Roblox Studio!

The magic behind all the amazing games in Roblox is called Roblox Studio. It's like your very own workshop where you can create, change, and make your game ideas come alive!

Here's why Roblox Studio is the best tool for young creators like you:

- *Easy to Use*: It's made just for you! Even if you've never made a game before, Roblox Studio has tools that are easy to understand and use.
- *Templates and Models:* Not sure where to start? There are pre-made items and game templates you can use. Want a castle? There's a model for that!
- *Make it Your Own*: You can customize every part of your game. Change colors, sizes, and add special effects—it's all up to you!
- *Test and Play*: Wondering how your game feels? You can play it right away and see. Test, make changes, and play again until it's perfect!

As you explore Roblox Studio, you'll discover how powerful it is. With all the tools available, your imagination is the only limit.

Is Roblox Studio Free?

Absolutely! Roblox Studio is like a free toy box for anyone who wants to create their own games. You can use it on your computer to make all sorts of amazing adventures. But guess what? If you want some extra special tools, there's a cool club called Roblox Developer Exchange (or RDX for short). This club has fancy tools for making super-duper games, but it might require payment. If you're new, start with the free stuff and explore more as you go!

Can I Use Roblox Studio on My Phone?

Nope! Roblox Studio is a big set of tools that needs a computer to work its magic. So, you'll need either a Windows computer or a Mac. But hey, you can still play Roblox games on your phone with the Roblox app!

Is Roblox Studio Only for Big Computers (PCs)?

No way! Whether you have a Windows PC or a shiny Mac, you can use Roblox Studio. Both are welcome in the world of Roblox!

Setting Up Roblox Studio: Step-by-Step

- Click on the Roblox Studio icon on your computer.
- If you have a Roblox account, type in your username and secret password. If you're new, click **"Sign Up"** to join the Roblox family.
- Fill in your details, choose a cool nickname, and make sure to remember your password. Oh, and don't forget to check your email too!
- Ta-da! You're now in Roblox Studio's main screen. Ready to start your game-making journey?
- To begin, click on the big **"New +"** button or go to **"File > New"**.
- You'll see a new game space where you can build whatever you dream of.

And if you ever feel lost or want to learn more, there's a special place called the Roblox Developer Hub filled with tips, tricks, and cool ideas to help you out. Have fun creating and playing games!

Introduction to the Roblox Studio Interface

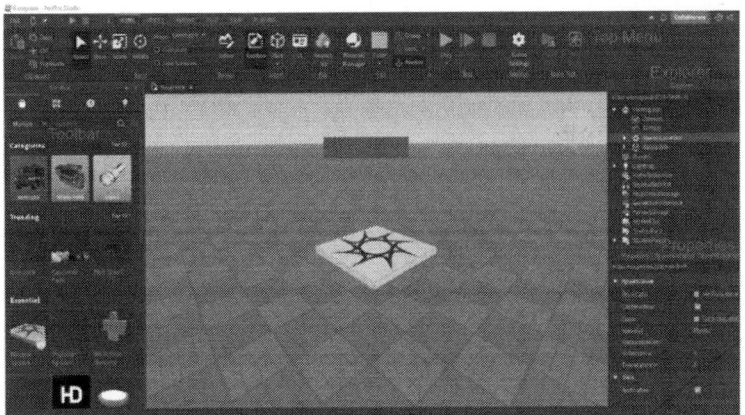

Hey there, future game makers! Let's explore the awesome parts of Roblox Studio together:

The Top Menu Bar

- **Location**: It's at the top, just like a superhero's cape!
- **What's cool about it**: It's like a magic wand with buttons. You can create your game, save your cool creations, and test out your new adventures. If you want to see some special panels, just head over to the View Menu.

The Explorer Panel

- **Location**: Look on the right side.
- **What's cool about it**: Think of it as a treasure map! It shows you all the items in your game—characters, trees, toys, and more. The things under 'Workspace' are what players will see in your game. There are also some secret folders like ServerStorage and StarterPlayer for advanced fun!

The Toolbox

- **Location**: Check out the left side.

- **What's cool about it**: It's like your very own toy box! Here, you'll find tools and toys made by other awesome creators. You can add fun characters, cool places, and groovy moves to your game.

The Properties Panel

- **Location**: Look at the bottom right.
- **What's cool about it**: It's like a magic mirror for your items. When you click on something, this panel tells you all about it—its name, size, and how it looks. You can change these to make them super unique!

The Viewport

- **Location**: It's the big area in the middle.
- **What's cool about it**: It's like your game's movie screen! You can watch your game come to life, walk around, and make sure everything is perfect.

And that's a quick tour of Roblox Studio! The more you play around, the more secrets and fun stuff you'll discover. So, roll up your sleeves, dive in, and start creating your dream games!

Your First Script: Hello, ROBLOX!

Are you excited to bring your Roblox characters and objects to life? Get ready to learn about scripting, which is like teaching your game elements to think and act on their own!

Let's start with your very first Roblox script. Our mission? To greet everyone with a cheerful "Hello, Roblox!" when they join your game. Follow these steps:

- *Open Roblox Studio:* Launch Roblox Studio and create a new game.

- *Insert a Part:* Go to the "Home" tab and click on "Part" to add a block into your game. This block will become our magical button.
- *Add a Script:* Click on the part you just added to select it. Then, in the "Model" tab, click on "PrimaryPart" and set it to "Part". Now, right-click on your part in the explorer, hover over "Insert Object", and choose "Script".
- *Writing Your Script:* Double-click on the new Script to open it. You'll see some default text, but let's focus on what's between script.Parent.Touched:Connect(function() and end). This is where the magic happens!

Now, type in the following code:

The Code
```
script.Parent.Touched:Connect(function()
    print("Hello, Roblox!")
end)
```

That's it! Save your script, and when someone touches the part you created, it will trigger the script to say "Hello, Roblox!" in the output window.

- *Test It Out:* Click the **"Play"** button. Walk your character over to the part and touch it. Look at the output panel, and you'll see our cheerful greeting!

Congratulations! You've written your first script. This is just the beginning. As you learn more about scripting, you can make platforms move, create fun in-game tools, and even spawn fireworks. The world of Roblox scripting is vast and exciting, waiting for you to explore and innovate!

Remember, every game you admire on Roblox started with that first line of code. With curiosity and persistence, you'll be crafting mesmerizing games and scripts in no time!

You're now on your way to becoming a Roblox scripter. Keep exploring, experimenting, and creating amazing experiences for everyone to enjoy in your games!

EMBRACING VARIABLES

Understanding Variables

Hey there, young coders! Let's talk about something super cool called variables. They're like special containers that can hold different things, just like your toy box!

Imagine you have a magical toy box that can transform its contents. Today, it's filled with action figures, and tomorrow, it might be bursting with puzzles. Well, in coding, a 'variable' is just like that magical toy box. It's a special name we give to store and keep track of different things!

What's in the Name?

Now, let's learn about choosing names for variables:

When we create a variable, we need to give it a name. Just like you name your toys, we give names to variables so we can remember what they hold. But there are some important rules to follow when choosing names:

- **Start with a letter**: The name of a variable must always begin with a letter of the alphabet.
- **Use letters and numbers**: You can use letters (both uppercase and lowercase) and numbers in your variable names. For example, you can have a variable named "myVariable123".
- **No spaces or special characters**: Avoid using spaces or special characters like !, @, #, $, %, etc. in your variable names. Stick to letters and numbers.
- **Be descriptive**: Choose names that describe what the variable represents. For example, if you're storing the number of points in a game, you could name your variable "score".

Remember, the name of a variable is like a label on your toy box. It helps you identify what's inside. So, choose names that make sense and are easy to understand.

Now that you know how to choose names for variables, you're ready to start using them in your code. Variables are super handy when you want to remember and use different values as you code. Have fun coding and exploring the world of variables!

Hey, young coders! Let's talk about choosing the perfect names for variables. It's like giving special names to your coding treasures!

Here are some tips for picking awesome variable names:

- Choose any name you want, like 'unicorn' or 'dragon', as long as it's not a secret word that coding languages like Lua already use.
- Just remember, names can't start with numbers. So '3dragons' is a no-no, but 'threeDragons' is perfect!
- Be careful with uppercase and lowercase letters. 'BlueSky' and 'bluesky' are different in coding!

Now, let's learn how to pick the BEST names for your variables:

- Always use full words. Instead of 'ab', use 'appleBanana'. It's like giving clear clues in a treasure hunt!
- For big and important things, like classes or categories, use 'BigFirstLetters'. For example, 'GoldenEgg'.
- For regular items or actions, use 'smallFirstLetterBigNextLetters'. So, 'jumpHigh' or 'runFast'.
- If something NEVER changes, like a rule in a game, SHOUT IT OUT with 'BIG_LETTERS'. For example, 'MAX_SCORE'.

- If there's a short group name inside a word, don't shout it all. So instead of 'HTMLFormat', go for 'htmlFormat'.

But wait, there are some names we can't use as variables:

There are special words in Lua that are already part of the coding language. They're like the crown jewels, so we can't use them as variable names. Here are some examples:

and

for

or

break

function

repeat

do

if

return

else

in

then

elseif

local

true

end

nil

until

false

not

while

And that's your guide to variables, my coding friends! Remember, coding is like a language. The more you play with it, the more fun stories and adventures you can create. So, keep naming those variables and see what exciting games you can craft!

Assigning Values

Let's learn how to assign values to variables. It's like giving special powers to your coding creations!

- To create a variable and give it a value, we use the = operator. The variable goes on the left, and the value goes on the right. If you don't give a value, it's like having an empty treasure chest.
- Variables can have two types of scopes: global and local. By default, variables have global scope, but it's usually better to make them local. Luau, the cool coding language we're using, can access local variables faster than global ones.
- To make a variable have local scope, we use the keyword "local" before the variable's name. It's like putting a secret lock on the treasure chest. This way, only the part of the code where we create the variable can use it.
- Remember, if you want to learn more about Scope in Luau, you can explore further to become an expert!

Now you have the power to assign values to variables and control their scope. So go ahead, try it out, and make your coding creations even more amazing!

```
local nilVar
local x = 10
local word = "Hello"
```

```
local reference = workspace.Camera
```

```
print(nilVar) -- nil
print(x) -- 10
print(word) -- Hello
```

Assigning Values to Multiple Variables

Imagine you have a few toy boxes and some toys you want to put inside them. Let's see how this works in the magical world of coding!

Filling Multiple Boxes:

- Imagine you have a Teddy and a Bunny. You can give both a toy in one quick move, like this:

```
Code
teddyBox = "Teddy"
bunnyBox = "Bunny"
```

So, Teddy gets a toy car and Bunny zooms away with a toy train!

When You Run Out of Toys:

- Let's imagine you said you have three toy boxes but only two toys:

```
Code
teddy, bunny, dino = "toy car", "toy train"
```

Oh no! Dino doesn't get anything. In coding, this is like Dino getting 'nil' which means an empty box.

When You Have Extra Toys:

- What if you have three toys but only two boxes?

```
Code
```

> teddy, bunny = "toy car", "toy train", "toy spaceship"

That cool spaceship doesn't have a box to go in! It just floats around in space.

Switching Toys Around :

- If you want Teddy to have a different toy, you just give him a new one! In coding, that's like saying:

```
Code
teddy = "toy rocket"
```

Now, Teddy zooms around with his new toy rocket, leaving the toy car behind. Easy peasy!

So, whether you're filling toy boxes or switching toys around, coding lets you play and imagine all sorts of fun stories! Keep playing and see where your adventures take you!

Now, let's imagine Teddy having so much fun with his new toy rocket. He's flying through the virtual skies, leaving his toy car behind. It's super easy to make these exciting things happen in the world of coding!

Whether you're filling toy boxes with different toys or switching toys around in your virtual world, coding gives you the power to play and imagine all kinds of fun stories. You can create amazing adventures and bring your wildest dreams to life!

So, keep exploring, coding, and letting your imagination run wild. Who knows where your coding adventures will take you? Have a blast and enjoy the magical world of Roblox!

```
local a, b, c = 1, 2, 3
local d, e, f = 4, 5-- extra variable
local g, h = 7, 8, 9-- extra value
```

```
print(a, b, c) -- 1, 2, 3
print(d, e, f) -- 4, 5, nil
print(g, h) -- 7, 8
```

Creating and Using Variables

Hey there, young magicians of coding! Today, we're going to explore the enchanting world of variables. They're like magical boxes that can hold all sorts of amazing things, like names, scores, colors, and more!

Example

Imagine you're watching a magician perform. They have a special hat that holds incredible surprises. Sometimes, they pull out a cute little rabbit named "Bobby," other times a beautiful bouquet of flowers, and maybe even a toy car! In coding, our variables are just like that magical hat, and whatever the magician pulls out represents the value inside the variable.

Now, let's embark on a coding adventure!

First, we need to create a variable. It's like giving a name to our very own magician's hat. We'll use a special coding language called Lua.

Check this example:

```
Code
local magicHat = "Bobby the Rabbit"
```

Ta-da! We've created a variable called magicHat, and inside it, we've placed the value "Bobby the Rabbit."

Let's imagine we're creating a soccer game, and we want to keep track of the players' scores. Every time a player scores a goal, we want to add a point to their score. It's just like a scoreboard in a soccer field!

Picture this: A soccer field with a scoreboard. As players score goals, the number on the scoreboard changes, showing their updated score.

With variables, we can do the same thing in coding! We'll create a variable to keep track of the player's score, and whenever they score a goal, we'll add a point to it.

Exciting, isn't it? You now have the power to create and use variables in your coding adventures. So go ahead, let your imagination soar, and create incredible programs filled with magic and wonder!

By using variables, you can create amazing games and interactive experiences. Whether it's a soccer game, an adventure in a virtual world, or anything else you can dream of, variables will help you keep track of important information and make your creations even more awesome!

So, grab your coding wand and get ready to cast some magical spells with variables. The possibilities are endless, and the only limit is your imagination. Have a fantastic time exploring the enchanting world of Roblox and coding!

Coding Time

Start With a Score of Zero

```
Code
local magicHat = "Bobby the Rabbit"
```

Adding Points:

we add a point to the count each time a goal is scored.

```
playerScore = playerScore + 1
```

Displaying the Score:

```
print("Goals scored: " .. playerScore)
```

Exercise: Creating a Countdown Timer:

Ready for some fun? Let's make a countdown for our soccer game. The game lasts 3 minutes, and we need to show how much time is left!

Illustration:

A big digital timer above the soccer field. It starts at 3:00 and counts down to 0:00.

Hey, soccer enthusiasts! Get ready to add some excitement to your game with a countdown timer. We'll create a virtual digital timer that will show how much time is left in the game. Cool, right?

Imagine a big digital timer displayed above the soccer field. It starts at 3:00, showing three minutes on the clock. As time passes, the numbers on the timer decrease until it reaches 0:00, indicating that the game is over.

To make this happen, we'll use the power of coding and variables. We'll create a special variable to hold the time left in the game. Every second, we'll decrease the value of the variable until it reaches zero.

Coding Exercise:

Starting the Timer

```
Code
local gameTime = 180 -- That's 3 minutes in seconds!
```

Making the Timer Tick:

We reduce the timer after each second

```
Code
for i = gameTime, 0, -1 do print("Time left: " .. i .. " seconds")
wait(1) end
```

End of the game:

The game ends as soon as the timer hits zero on its counter.

```
Code
print("Game Over! Final Score: " .. playerScore)
```

BRINGING WORLDS TO LIFE WITH INSTANCES

Introducing Instances: Objects in Your Game

Hey there, young coders! Let's dive into the exciting world of Object-Oriented Programming, or OOP for short. It's like having a super cool toy organizer for your playroom, keeping all your code neat and easy to find, just like your toys!

What's an Object?

You've played with objects before, like Lego bricks or toy cars, right? Well, in coding, we call those objects too! They're like special tools that help us create amazing things in programs, just like the magical tools in Roblox!

Why is OOP Cool for Me?

But what exactly is an object? Imagine you have a toy box labeled 'Super Cars'. Inside, you have awesome toy cars, stickers to decorate them, and maybe even some instructions on how to race them. In coding, that toy box is an object. It's a special container that holds both the toys, which we call data, and ways to play with them, which we call functions.

Racing Game Example

Now, let's talk about why OOP is super cool for you! Think about when you play with a remote-controlled car. You just press the buttons, and the car zooms around without you needing to know how the engine works or how the remote sends signals. This idea, where you can enjoy playing without knowing all the tiny details, is called 'abstraction'. And OOP helps us with that!

Imagine you're creating an incredible racing game. How awesome would it be if you could simply say, "Magic, bring me a new race car!", and poof, a shiny new car appears in the game? That's exactly what OOP allows you to do! With OOP, you can command your game as if you're casting magical spells!

Let's Create Magic in Code!

Now, let's create some magic in code! In the wonderful language of Lua, we can create our very own objects. For our racing game, a car object might be a special box that holds its color, speed, and even some cool tricks it can perform.

So, my young magicians of coding, get ready to create some amazing objects and bring magic to your programs! Let your imagination run wild and see what incredible things you can make happen!

Get your coding wands ready and let's cast some coding spells! It's time to create objects that will bring your games and programs to life. With OOP, you'll have the power to make things happen with just a few lines of code. So, jump in and let the magic unfold!

```
Code
car = {"RacePosition" = "3", "Speed" = 50, "Driver" = "Guest12372", "WorldPosition" = vector(25.31, 3.23, 53.86)}
```

Get ready for an exciting adventure into the world of cars and functions. Fasten your seatbelts because we're about to embark on an awesome ride!

Imagine you have a collection of toy cars. Each car is like a special table that holds different values at different spots, depending on where it is. It's just like having a race track where each car has its own unique features and position.

Now, let's create something really cool - a function that will allow us to create new cars. Think of it as having our very own special tool, just like the magical *Instance.new()* function we use in coding. We'll call this function "*newCar*," and it will take in important information like the car's position, the driver's name, and the car's model.

But wait, having functions all by themselves isn't very exciting in the coding world. So, in Lua, we'll gather all our functions inside a special table called Car. This table will be like a garage that holds all the functions related to the Car object. We chose the name "*Car*" because, well, it's all about cars, of course!

By organizing our functions in this way, our code becomes much more organized and easier to manage. Plus, it's a lot of fun to work with!

So, my young coding enthusiasts, let's rev up our engines and take a look at how our code will look with this awesome Car table containing all the car-related functions. Get ready to unleash your creativity as we explore the world of coding and cars together!

Here it is

```
Car = {}

function Car.newCar(position, driver, model)
```

```
    -- Code to create a new car goes here
End
```

It's important to make our car-related functions easy to find and use whenever we need them.

To do that, we'll gather all these special functions inside something called the Car table. Imagine it as a special toolbox that holds everything we need to create and control cars in our program. This way, we won't have to search all over the place to find the right tools.

Now, imagine you're sitting in the driver's seat, ready to create some amazing cars using our *newCar* function and the awesome Car table. It's like you're the master car designer, bringing your wildest ideas to life!

Remember, coding is all about being creative and solving problems. So, let your imagination soar and have a fantastic time creating incredible cars and going on exciting adventures with your code!

Sometimes, code can look a little tricky to read. But don't worry, we have a special trick up our sleeve called Lua syntax. It's like having some magical candy that makes our code easier to understand. By using this special syntax, our code will look even more friendly and readable.

So, my young coding wizards, get ready to embark on a coding journey where you'll create awesome cars, solve puzzles, and have tons of fun along the way. Let's dive in and make some coding magic happen!

Code
```
Car = {}
```

```
function Car.new(position, driver, model)

end

function Car.new(position, driver, model)

end
```

Code

```
print("Game Over! Final Score: " .. playerScore)
```

Wow, that looks much better! Just by looking at the code, we can easily understand what the function is meant to do. It's all about creating new objects, and we have a special name for this kind of function. It's called a constructor. This constructor function is responsible for constructing new Car objects. How cool is that? Programmers have such creative names!

By the way, there's something else we should know. There's a special group called a class, and in this case, it's called Car. The class Car is like a blueprint that tells us how to make Car objects. The constructor and other functions inside the Car class are what make it special. And those objects we create using the constructor? Well, those are the actual cars themselves!

Since each Car object is just like a table, we need to create a new table and put all the important information inside it. Think of it like building a car from scratch, putting in all the necessary parts to make it work.

So, my awesome young coders, now you know how this code creates new Car objects. It's like being a master builder, assembling cars with all the right pieces. Let's keep exploring and discover more exciting things in the world of coding and Roblox!

Code

```
Car = {}

function Car.new(position, driver, model)

    local newcar = {}

    newcar.Position = position

    newcar.Driver = driver

    newcar.Model = model

    return newcar

end
```

Imagine you have a special table called Car that holds all the information about different cars. But there's a little problem! Our Car table is organized, but it needs some special powers to do amazing things with our cars.

So, instead of putting the functions directly into the Car table, we have a better way to make things tidy and efficient. We can create the functions separately and let Lua, our coding language, know where to find them when it needs to do something special with a car.

Let's say you want to find out who the driver of a car is. Normally, you would write something like driver = *Car.Driver*. Lua will look inside the Car table and find the driver information right away. It's like having a clear path to the information we need, without any extra clutter!

But how does this magic work? That's where meta-tables come in. Meta-tables are special tables that have methods or functions to perform special tasks on other tables. And one of these special tasks is exactly what we need: the .__index metamethod.

When Lua searches for something in a table but doesn't find it (which means it's nil or empty), the .__index metamethod comes to the rescue. It helps us redirect Lua to another table that has all the special functions we need. And guess what? Our Car table is that magical table!

I won't go into too much detail about meta-tables right now, as it can get a bit tricky. But just remember that meta-tables allow us to make our code even more powerful and organized.

So, my young coding wizards, get ready to unleash the magic of meta-tables in your code! Let your creativity soar as you create incredible tables, add functions to them, and make your programs even more awesome! It's time to bring your code to life and have a blast in the world of Roblox!

Code

```
Car = {}

Car.__index = Car

function Car.new(position, driver, model)

    local newcar = {}

    setmetatable(newcar, Car)

    newcar.Position = position

    newcar.Driver = driver

    newcar.Model = model

    return newcar

end
```

Now, here's something interesting! Suppose we use the code *newcar = Car.New()* to create a new car. If we try to use a function on the *newcar*, it will search through the Car table as well, not just the *newcar*.

To make our *newcar* even more useful, let's add a special function to it. This function will give our *newcar* some superpowers and make it capable of doing awesome things!

Imagine having a function that lets our *newcar* do incredible tricks, like zooming around the track, honking its horn, or even changing its color. It's like giving our *newcar* a secret code to unlock its hidden abilities!

By adding this function to our *newcar* object, we can make it even more exciting and interactive. We'll have the power to control and customize our *newcar* in all sorts of creative ways.

So, my amazing young coders, let's get ready to add some fantastic functions to our *newcar* objects. With these functions, we'll have the power to make our cars do incredible things in our Roblox adventures. Get ready to code some magic and enjoy the thrill of creating and controlling your very own virtual cars!

Code

```
Car = {}
Car.__index = Car
function Car.new(position, driver, model)
    local newcar = {}
    setmetatable(newcar, Car)
```

```
    newcar.Position = position
    newcar.Driver = driver
    newcar.Model = model
    return newcar
end
function Car:Boost()
    self.Speed = self.Speed + 5
end
Now we can do.
newcar = Car.new(Vector3.new(1,0,1), "Guest1892", game.ReplicatedStorage.F1Car)
newcar:Boost()
```

When we make a new car in our game and want to make it go faster, we use a special function *called :Boost()*. But have you ever wondered how it actually works behind the scenes? Let me explain it to you in a way that feels magical!

Imagine we have a new car object called newcar. When we call *newcar:Boost()*, something really interesting happens. In Roblox, we use a coding language called Lua. Lua tries to find the Boost function inside the newcar object, but oops, it's not there!

But don't worry, Lua has a clever trick! It looks at the special meta-table of *newcar*, which is like a secret library of functions that can help our car. Lua then tries to find the Boost function inside the Car table, which is stored in the meta-table of *newcar*. And guess what? It finds it there! How cool is that?

Now, let's talk about a neat feature in Lua. If we write a function like *table:Method()*, something magical happens. Lua automatically gives us a special word called self. It's like having a helper that knows exactly which object we're talking about. It's the same as writing *table.Method(self)*, but in a shorter and more magical way!

Remember when we talked about *boop:Beep()* being the same as calling *boop.Beep(boop)?* Well, the self word is the key to that magic! It passes the object itself to the function, allowing the function to perform actions specifically on that individual object. And that's exactly what happens when we *use :Boost()*. It makes each car go faster by increasing its speed.

So, my coding wizards, get ready to create awesome cars, boost their speed, and watch them zoom around in your Roblox games! Let your imagination run wild and have a blast creating incredible experiences for yourself and others to enjoy.

Integrating with Module Scripts

Remember our magical toy organizer, OOP? And those special toy boxes called 'objects'? Now, let's introduce another magical scroll called the 'module script'. Think of this script as a spell book in a wizard's library. When we combine OOP with module scripts, our magic becomes even stronger!

Code

```
--module script called Car in game.ReplicatedStorage
Car = {}
Car.__index = Car
function Car.new(position, driver, model)
    local newcar = {}
    setmetatable(newcar, Car)
    newcar.Position = position
```

```
    newcar.Driver = driver
    newcar.Model = model
    return newcar
end
function Car:Boost()
    self.Speed = self.Speed + 5
end
return Car
--main script
Car = require(game.ReplicatedStorage.Car)
newcar = Car.new()
newcar:Boost()
```

This gives you a way of neatly splitting potentially big scripts into little chunks which are easy to understand and change if needed.

What about Inheritance

Hey there, fellow young coders and toy lovers! Let's go on an exciting adventure where we explore the concept of "inheritance" using our favorite toys: cars and trucks!

Imagine you have a treasure chest filled with incredible toy cars. They can race, zoom, and do all sorts of fun things. But one day, you receive a brand new toy: a super cool truck! This truck is like a car, but it has some extra special features that make it unique and awesome.

Now, in the magical world of coding, we have a special trick called "*inheritance*." It's like borrowing some magical powers from one toy and giving them to another. Instead of creating a whole new truck toy from scratch, we can use the cool things our cars can do and share those powers with our truck. It's like spreading the magic!

So, how does this magical inheritance work? Well, imagine our toy cars as special spells. When we want to create our new truck spell, we don't have to start from scratch. We simply say, "Hey, truck! Remember all the cool things cars can do? You can do them too!" And just like that, with a wave of our magical wand, our truck now has all the magical powers of a car, plus some extra truck magic!

Making Our Magical Truck

Now, it's time to create our very own magical truck spell! Our truck is similar to a car, but it has some special power-ups. Maybe it can jump super high or carry a mountain of toys. To make our truck spell, we'll use the power of inheritance. We'll give our truck all the cool features of a car and then add in our unique truck magic. It's like mixing all the best ingredients together to create something truly extraordinary!

So, my fellow coding wizards and toy enthusiasts, let's use the magic of inheritance to create amazing trucks with superpowers! Combine the best features of cars and add your own special touches to make your trucks the most magical toys in the universe!

```
Code
Truck = {}
Truck.__index = Truck
function Truck.new(position, driver, model, powerup)
    local newtruck = {}
```

```
        setmetatable(newtruck, Truck)
        return newtruck
end
return Truck
```

If we followed this approach, we would still have to include all the code for declaring the car inside the constructor. This can be quite repetitive and unnecessary. Instead, a better solution is to simply create a car object directly inside the constructor.

```
Code
Car = require(game.ReplicatedStorage.Car)

Truck = {}

Truck.__index = Truck

function Truck.new(position, driver, model, powerup)
    local newtruck = Car.new(position, driver, model)
    setmetatable(newtruck, Truck)
    newtruck.Powerup = powerup
    return newtruck
end
return Truck
```

Imagine you have an awesome toy truck that you want to make zoom super fast with a magical "Boost" button. Sometimes, when you press that button, you might hear a little "Oops! I can't find the Boost magic." But don't worry, because I have a clever solution to make our truck go zoom!

The Search for Boost Magic

Right now, our truck is searching high and low, trying to find that special Boost magic. But it's having trouble finding it immediately. So, what can we do to help our truck out? Well, I have a magical trick called a 'metatable' that will come to the rescue!

The Speedy Toy Car with Boost Magic

Imagine we have another amazing toy car that's really speedy. This car knows the secret of the Boost magic! We'll tell our truck, "Hey, remember that speedy toy car we played with before? It has the Boost magic! Let's borrow it!" That's where our metatable comes in. It's like a magical signpost that points our truck in the right direction, guiding it to the Boost magic from the toy car.

Now, with this special trick, our toy truck becomes even more amazing! It can zoom around super fast, all thanks to the Boost magic it borrowed from our toy car friend. Just imagine pressing the Boost button and watching your toy truck take off with lightning speed!

Always remember, my friend, that with a sprinkle of imagination, we can make any toy do super cool stuff! Whether it's a truck, a car, or even a magical creature, our imagination can take us on incredible adventures and bring our toys to life in the most exciting ways. So, let your creativity soar and have fun exploring the magical world of Roblox coding!

Code

```
Car = require(game.ReplicatedStorage.Car)

Truck = {}

Truck.__index = Truck

setmetatable(Truck, Car)

function Truck.new(position, driver, model, powerup)
```

```
    local newtruck = Car.new(position, driver, model)

    setmetatable(newtruck, Truck)

    newtruck.Powerup = powerup

    return newtruck

end

return Truck
```

Let's embark on an exciting journey and unleash our creativity with an incredible toy truck. And guess what? We're going to make it zoom super fast with a magical "Boost" button! But sometimes, our truck might encounter a little hiccup and say, "Oops! I can't find the Boost magic." Don't worry, because I have a secret plan to make it work!

The Quest for Boost Magic

Our toy truck is on a quest, searching high and low for that special boost. However, it may not find it right away. So, what's the secret? Let me share it with you! Remember that amazing toy car we played with before? The one that's super speedy? Well, it holds the knowledge of the Boost magic! We'll ask our truck to remember that car and borrow its magical power. Isn't that cool?

Unleashing the Metatable Trick

To bring this magic to life, we'll use a special trick called a 'metatable.' It's like a secret map that guides our truck in the right direction, leading it straight to the Boost magic hidden within the toy car. With this clever trick, our toy truck will become even more incredible!

Zooming with Boost Magic

Now, our toy truck can zoom around at lightning speed, all thanks to the incredible Boost magic it borrowed from our toy car friend. It's like having a turbo boost that makes our truck the coolest and speediest toy on the block!

Ignite Your Imagination

Always remember, my friend, that with a sprinkle of imagination, we can make any toy do remarkable things! Whether it's a truck, a car, or any other toy you can imagine, our creativity holds the key to endless fun and excitement.

So, get ready for fantastic adventures in the world of coding and play! Create amazing games, bring your toys to life, and embrace the magic of Roblox. Let your imagination soar as you explore the limitless possibilities that await you. It's time to have a blast and make unforgettable memories!

LOOPING ADVENTURES

Welcome, my young magicians and future coding wizards! Imagine yourself as a talented magician who has just discovered a marvelous spell. This spell has the power to make a toy car zoom across the room. But here's the exciting part: you want the car to go back and forth, again and again! Instead of casting the spell repeatedly, wouldn't it be amazing if there was a magic trick to make the spell repeat on its own? Get ready to enter the enchanting world of loops!

The Marvel of Loops

So, what exactly are loops? Think of them as magical circles that you can create. When you cast a spell inside this circle, it doesn't happen just once; it keeps happening over and over, as many times as you wish! It's like the spell gets caught in a loop, playing on repeat until you decide to stop it.

Unleashing the Power of Loops

With loops, you hold the power to make your magic spells perform incredible tricks. You can make the toy car zoom back and forth endlessly, creating a mesmerizing motion that will leave everyone in awe. It's like having a never-ending show of magic right at your fingertips!

Embrace the Magic of Loops

So, my young magicians and future coding wizards, loops are your secret weapons to bring your spells to life and create amazing experiences. Embrace the magic of loops, experiment with different patterns and repetitions, and let your imagination soar as you make your toys dance to the rhythm of your spells.

Unleash Your Creativity

Remember, coding is all about exploring, discovering, and having fun. So, grab your wand, cast your loops, and let the magic unfold before your eyes! Enjoy the journey of coding, where you can create incredible experiences and bring your wildest imaginations to life. Embrace the power of loops and let your coding adventures begin!

Code
```
for i = 1, 10 do
print("Zoom, zoom, zoom!")
end
```

This code tells the car to zoom 10 times!

This code snippet is all about instructing the car to zoom ten times in Roblox! But have you ever wondered why loops are so cool and why we use them in coding? Let me explain.

The Magic of Loops

Imagine having to clap your hands a hundred times. That would be quite tiring, right? But with loops, it's like having a magical helper that does the clapping for you. You simply tell it how many times you want the action to be repeated, and it takes care of the rest!

Loops in Roblox

In the world of Roblox, loops play a crucial role in programming. We often use loops to repeat actions, creating fascinating effects in our games and experiences. For example, you can use a loop to make a door open and close continuously, or to make a light blink on and off. The possibilities are endless!

By harnessing the power of loops in Roblox, you can automate repetitive tasks and add dynamic elements to your creations. Whether you want to create a bustling city with cars zooming by or a magical world where objects come to life, loops will be your trusty companions along the way.

So, as you dive into the exciting realm of Roblox programming, remember that loops are your secret weapon to make things happen repeatedly and bring your ideas to life. Embrace the power of loops, experiment with different patterns and durations, and watch your creations come alive with captivating animations and interactions.

Now, let's get coding and unlock the infinite possibilities that loops offer in the enchanting world of Roblox!

```
Code
while true do

door.Open = not door.Open

wait(2)

end
```

Get ready, my creative friends, because we're about to uncover a super cool trick that will make our toys come alive! You know those smooth movements you see in cartoons? Well, we can create our very own animations in Roblox using a special technique called loops. It's time to let our toys groove and show off their moves!

Creating Awesome Animations

Let's walk through the steps of creating our fantastic animations together. Imagine you have a toy robot as your character. Now, let's give it some cool moves!

Step 1: Pick Your Character

First, choose your toy robot or any other character you'd like to animate. This will be the star of your animation, so choose wisely and get ready for some fun!

Step 2: Decide on Movement

Think about what you want your robot to do. Does it wave its hand as a friendly greeting? Maybe it can dance or jump! Decide on the movement you want to bring to life in your animation.

Step 3: Loop It!

Now comes the exciting part! We'll use a special loop to make the robot perform its movement again and again. It's like the robot is saying "Hello!" over and over with its waving hand or performing any other action you've chosen.

With this loop, our robot will keep repeating its movement forever, creating a fantastic animation that will bring joy to everyone who sees it!

Unleash Your Imagination

So, my imaginative coders and toy enthusiasts, let's dive into the enchanting world of animation and bring our toys to life! Get ready to create magical movements, make characters dance, wave, or do anything you can dream of. The possibilities are endless!

Remember, coding is like a secret language that unlocks the hidden powers of your imagination. So, have fun, experiment, and let your creativity shine as you create amazing animations that will make your toys sparkle like stars!

You are the director of your own animated adventures, my young wizards of coding and play. Let the magic of loops guide you as you bring your toys to life in the most incredible ways imaginable. Get ready to dazzle the world with your animated creations!

```
for i = 1, 5 do
robot.WaveHand()
wait(1)
end
```

This makes the robot wave its hand five times, with a little pause in between!

Make it Smooth with Tweening

Tweening is a fancy word for smoothly changing something over time. With tweening and loops, our animations look super smooth!

```
local tweenService = game:GetService("TweenService")
local waveTween = tweenService:Create(robot.Hand, TweenInfo.new(1), {Position = robot.Hand.Position + Vector3.new(0,5,0)})
for i = 1, 3 do
waveTween:Play()
wait(1.5)
end
```

Now our robot doesn't just wave; it waves with style!

Looping Through Instances

Have you ever wandered through the marvelous worlds of Roblox? They are filled with breathtaking sights like trees, flowers, and fluffy clouds. Now, picture this: what if we could make all the flowers in a beautiful garden bloom simultaneously? Well, I've got fantastic news for you! We have a magical trick called loops that can turn this dream into a reality.

Understanding Instances in Roblox

In Roblox, we have something called instances. Think of them as individual toys within our game. Now, imagine each flower in our garden as a special instance. With the power of loops, we can communicate with all these flower instances at once and create something truly magical!

How Looping Magic Works

Here's the secret recipe: we will use a loop to send a special message to each flower instance in the garden. It's like whispering a secret code to all the flowers, saying, "Hey, it's time to bloom!" And just like that, all the flowers will listen to our magical command and bloom together, turning the garden into a vibrant paradise of colors and fragrances. It will be an awe-inspiring sight!

The Conductor's Baton of Loops

Remember, my young coders and nature enthusiasts, loops are like a conductor's baton in an orchestra. They help us coordinate and synchronize all the flowers, making them dance to the same beautiful tune.

Embark on an Enchanting Journey

So, let's embark on this enchanting journey of coding and nature! Explore the vast worlds of Roblox, uncover the wonders they hold, and use loops to create breathtaking experiences. Make the flowers bloom, the trees sway, and the clouds float across the sky, all with the power of your imagination and coding skills.

Let your creativity blossom, my young wizards of code and nature. With loops as your guide, you can create mesmerizing scenes that will captivate anyone who steps foot into your virtual garden. Get ready to unleash the magic of loops and bring the beauty of nature to life in the extraordinary realm of Roblox!

```
Code
for _, flower in pairs(garden:GetChildren()) do
if flower:IsA("Flower") then
flower.Bloom()
end
end
```

This code tells every flower in the garden to bloom!

Example: Animated Obstacle Course

Obstacle courses are a thrilling challenge, but what if we took them to the next level? Imagine an obstacle course that not only puts your skills to the test but also keeps you on your toes with moving and changing obstacles! With the power of loops, we can create dynamic obstacles that require quick thinking and lightning-fast reflexes to overcome.

Let's explore three exhilarating examples of dynamic obstacles that will inject excitement into your obstacle course:

Moving Platforms:

Get ready for a heart-pounding challenge! Introduce moving platforms that slide from side to side. These platforms will add an extra layer of complexity to your course. By leveraging loops, we can animate these platforms to glide back and forth, creating an ever-shifting path that demands precision and agility. Players will have to time their jumps and movements perfectly to navigate across these moving platforms. Are you up for the challenge?

```
Code
while true do

platform:MoveTo(platform.Position + Vector3.new(5,0,0))

wait(2)

platform:MoveTo(platform.Position - Vector3.new(5,0,0))

wait(2)

end
```

Spinning Blades:

Prepare for an adrenaline rush! Incorporate spinning blades that rotate continuously. These formidable obstacles will keep players on their toes as they try to avoid getting caught. By utilizing loops, we can bring these spinning blades to life, creating a thrilling sense of danger. Players will need to be nimble and react swiftly, timing their movements precisely to slip through the gaps between the blades. Can you conquer the spinning blades and emerge victorious?

```
Code
while true do
```

```
blade.Orientation = blade.Orientation + Vector3.new(0,10,0)
wait(0.1)
end
```

Popping Obstacles:

Get ready to be surprised! Introduce popping obstacles that unexpectedly emerge from the ground. These surprises will test players' reflexes and observation skills. With loops, we can animate these obstacles to pop up at random intervals, keeping players on edge and requiring them to stay alert. Players will need to react quickly and adapt to these sudden obstacles to avoid being caught off guard. Will you stay one step ahead of the popping surprises?

With the power of loops, we can breathe life into these dynamic obstacles, transforming your obstacle course into an unforgettable experience. Players will need to think quickly, react swiftly, and adapt on the fly to conquer these ever-changing challenges.

So, my adventurous course designers and thrill-seeking players, let your creativity soar as you incorporate moving platforms, spinning blades, and popping obstacles into your dynamic obstacle courses. With loops as your ally, you can create an exhilarating world full of excitement and challenge. Get ready to push your limits and bring your obstacle courses to life in extraordinary ways!

```
Code
for i = 1, 3 do
obstacle:PopOut()
wait(1)
obstacle:Hide()
```

```
wait(2)
end
```

Get Ready to Rock the Dance Floor with Loops!

Are you ready to have an absolute blast? It's time to unleash the power of loops and throw the most incredible dance party for our Roblox characters! Get ready to show off your groovy moves and create a dance floor that will transport everyone to a world of pure excitement!

Let's break down the steps to ensure our dance party is an absolute hit:

Step 1: Pick the Dance Floor:

Imagine a dance floor that's not just cool, but super cool! Picture a floor filled with mesmerizing lights, creating a disco atmosphere that will instantly set the stage for an epic dance-off. When our characters step on this magical floor, it will light up and become the center of attention. Get ready to create a dance floor that's out of this world!

Step 2: Choose the Dances:

Now it's time to decide which awesome dance moves our characters will showcase. Will they breakdance with jaw-dropping flips and spins? Perhaps they'll glide across the floor with the iconic moonwalk, channeling the spirit of the legendary Michael Jackson. The choice is yours! You can even include the robot dance or incorporate graceful twirls. Let your imagination run wild and come up with all the dance moves you can think of. This is your chance to create a dance experience like no other!

Step 3: Start the Loop:

Here comes the exciting part! We'll use loops to make the dance moves change randomly, adding an element of surprise to the party. It's like having a dance generator that keeps everyone guessing. Each time the loop repeats, our characters will seamlessly transition to a different dance move, keeping the energy high and the party exhilarating. Get ready for a dance floor that's always full of surprises!

So, put on your dancing shoes and get ready to groove! With loops as our secret weapon, our Roblox characters will dance like never before, creating an electrifying atmosphere that will make everyone want to join in. Remember, my young party planners and coding enthusiasts, dancing is all about self-expression, having fun, and spreading joy. Let your creativity shine as you choreograph the most incredible dance moves for your characters. Make them dance to the beat of your imagination!

Get ready for a dance party like no other, filled with laughter, music, and endless fun. Let's harness the power of loops to create a dance extravaganza that will bring our Roblox world alive with rhythm and excitement! So, turn up the music, gather your friends, and let's dance our way into an unforgettable experience!

Code

```
local dances = {"breakdance", "moonwalk", "robot", "twirl"}
while true do
local randomDance = dances[math.random(1, #dances)]
character:DoDance(randomDance)
wait(3)
end
```

Get ready for a dance party that never stops! With the power of loops, our characters will effortlessly pick a random dance move every 3 seconds, ensuring the excitement never fades. Let's dive into the world of loop magic once again and continue our coding adventures!

Loops are like the magic wands of coding, allowing us to repeat actions as many times as we desire with just a flick, swish, and swirl. They give us the power to create endless possibilities and keep the excitement going strong. Are you ready to unleash your coding skills and explore more thrilling adventures? Let's delve into the world of loops and see where our creativity takes us!

With each iteration of the loop, our characters will dynamically select a new dance move, adding an element of surprise and keeping the dance party in full swing. It's like having a dance DJ that never misses a beat! So, embrace the magic of loops, let your imagination soar, and witness the dance party that never ceases to amaze.

Get ready for more coding adventures as we continue to harness the power of loops. With a wave of our coding wands, we can create incredible experiences and explore new horizons. So, let's keep the loop magic going and unlock the endless possibilities of coding!

Remember, my aspiring coders and dance enthusiasts, loops are your trusty companions in the world of coding. They allow you to repeat actions, create dynamic experiences, and infuse your projects with excitement. So, let your coding skills shine and let the loop magic guide you to even greater coding adventures!

MAKING CHOICES WITH CONDITIONAL STATEMENTS

Introduction to Magic Choices in Roblox

Are you ready, my young adventurers, to embark on a journey filled with enchantment? Close your eyes and imagine yourself in a land where magic abounds. Right before you, there's a mysterious chest, beckoning you to open it. But here's the twist: only if you possess the golden key will the chest reveal its hidden treasures! Without the key, it remains locked, safeguarding its secrets.

This magical chest works just like what we programmers call a 'conditional statement' in Roblox. It's akin to setting up special rules in a game, where different choices lead to different outcomes. Now, let's unveil the magic spell of the conditional statement!

So, what exactly is a conditional statement? Think of it as a powerful decision-making spell in the realm of coding. It grants you the ability to check if something is true or false and, based on that, make decisions on what action to take. It's like having your own wizardry powers to make choices!

Now, let's dive deeper into the magic of the "IF" spell. Much like our magical chest, the if statement in Roblox checks for something specific. You can imagine it as a guardian stationed at the entrance of a secret clubhouse, requesting a special password before granting entry. Only if you provide the correct password will the door swing open, welcoming you inside.

In the realm of coding, the "IF" spell is written in a unique way. It resembles a secret code that instructs the computer on what to do based on certain conditions. It's like giving commands to the magical forces of Roblox!

Decoding the Magic Spell: Conditional Statement

So, my clever young coders and aspiring wizards, get ready to unleash the power of conditional statements in your coding adventures. Just like a magician, you possess the ability to establish rules and make choices that lead to different outcomes. The magic of coding is within your grasp!

Using If Statements for Decision Making

Remember, coding is a magical language that allows you to create incredible things. So, let your imagination soar, experiment with different conditions, and witness as your code brings the world of Roblox to life!

Now, open your eyes and let the magical coding journey begin! The treasures of knowledge and creativity await you as you unravel the mysteries of conditional statements and forge your own magical experiences in the realm of Roblox.

```
Code
if youHaveGoldenKey == true then
chest:Open()
end
```

Welcome to the realm of Roblox programming, where the magic of "if" statements brings your games to life! Let's explore how this powerful tool can create exciting interactions and add a touch of enchantment to your Roblox adventures.

The Power of "If" in Games

With the "if" statement, you can create a myriad of cool interactions in your Roblox games. Imagine this: if a player reaches a certain score, they unlock a special ability! Or, if they discover a hidden item, a secret door opens, revealing a whole new world of surprises.

Creating Game Interactions with "If-Else" Statements

Now, let's delve into the magic of the "if-else" spell. In certain situations, the magical land may require more than one decision. That's where the "if-else" statement comes in handy. Picture this: if you have the golden key, the chest opens, but if you don't have the key, the chest stays locked and provides a friendly message.

The Magic of the "IF-ELSE" Spell

The "if-else" spell is like having a versatile enchantment at your disposal. It allows you to perform different actions based on the conditions you set. With this spell, you can create branching paths in your games, offering unique experiences and interactions depending on the choices made by the players.

So, my aspiring Roblox programmers, let your creativity flow and weave the magic of "if" and "if-else" statements into your games. Imagine the possibilities: players making decisions that shape their journey, unlocking hidden treasures or encountering delightful surprises along the way.

Remember, coding is like wielding a wand of possibilities. So, experiment with different conditions, triggers, and outcomes. Let your imagination soar as you create games that captivate and engage players in the magical world of Roblox.

Now, go forth and embrace the power of "if" and "if-else" statements in your Roblox programming journey. The realm of endless creativity and enchanting gameplay awaits you!

Here's how the enhanced magic spell looks:

Code
```
if youHaveGoldenKey == true then
chest:Open()
else
print("Find the golden key to unlock the treasures!")
end
```

Embark on Exciting Adventures with If-Else in Roblox!

Welcome to the world of Roblox programming, where the power of if-else statements allows you to create dynamic and immersive gameplay experiences. Let's dive into the possibilities and learn how if-else statements can add depth and excitement to your Roblox games.

Example: Day and Night Cycle

Let's bring the sun and moon to life in your game through the magic of decision-making. With if-else statements, we can create a captivating day and night cycle that adds realism and atmosphere to your Roblox world.

Imagine this: as the game time reaches a certain point, the sun gracefully sets, and the moon takes its place in the sky. Here's the spell that will make it happen:

Code
```
if gameTime >= sunsetTime then
    -- Set the sun's visibility to false and the moon's visibility to true
    sun.Visible = false
    moon.Visible = true
else
    -- Set the sun's visibility to true and the moon's visibility to false
    sun.Visible = true
```

```
    moon.Visible = false
end
```

In this enchanting spell, we use an if-else statement to check if the game time has reached the designated sunset time. If it has, we make the sun disappear by setting its visibility to false, while the moon gracefully takes its place by setting its visibility to true. On the other hand, if the game time hasn't reached the sunset time, we ensure the sun remains visible and the moon stays hidden.

By weaving this spell into your game's code, you can create a mesmerizing day and night cycle that adds depth and immersion to your Roblox world. Players will experience the passage of time as they journey through your game, marveling at the beauty of the transitioning skies.

Remember, my aspiring Roblox programmers and game creators, if-else statements are your magical tools for creating dynamic interactions and captivating gameplay. Experiment with different conditions and outcomes, and let your imagination guide you as you craft unique experiences for your players.

Now, go forth and unleash the power of if-else statements in your Roblox adventures. The realm of endless possibilities awaits you!

```
Code
local gameTime = workspace.CurrentTime

if gameTime >= 18 then

world:TurnToNight()

elseif gameTime <= 6 then

world:TurnToMorning()

else
```

```
world:BrightSunnyDay()
end
```

As a skilled Roblox programmer and instructor, I'm here to guide you on an exciting journey into the realm of conditional spells. With these powerful tools, you can create captivating choose-your-own-adventure games where each decision leads to a unique and magical story. Let's embark on this adventure together!

Challenge: Building a Choose-Your-Adventure Game

Get ready to unleash your creativity and craft your very own magical tale with a choose-your-own-adventure game. In this challenge, players will be immersed in a world of enchantment, where their decisions shape the course of their journey. Let's break it down into two steps:

- **Start the Adventure**: Begin by welcoming the player and presenting them with the first choice. It could be something like choosing a character or deciding which path to take. This sets the stage for the magical tale that is about to unfold.
- **Use the if-else Spell**: Now, here's where the real magic happens. Depending on the player's choice, you'll take them on a different journey, where their decisions lead to unique outcomes. Use the if-else spell to create branching paths and captivating storylines. For example, if the player chooses to explore a mysterious cave, they may encounter hidden treasures, while if they decide to venture into the enchanted forest, they might encounter mythical creatures.

By leveraging the power of conditional spells, you can weave a tapestry of magical adventures, offering players endless possibilities and an immersive gameplay experience.

Remember, dear wizards of Roblox, each decision the player makes should have consequences, shaping their adventure and revealing different facets of the magical world you create. Use your coding skills to bring these choices to life and watch as your players become the heroes of their own stories.

Now, embrace the challenge, unleash your creativity, and let the magic of conditional spells guide you as you build your very own choose-your-own-adventure game in Roblox. May your imagination soar and your coding skills shine as you create a truly enchanting experience for your players.

Code
```
local playerChoice = game:AskPlayer("Do you want to enter the enchanted forest or the spooky cave?")

if playerChoice == "enchanted forest" then

game:StartEnchantedJourney()

elseif playerChoice == "spooky cave" then

game:StartSpookyAdventure()

else

print("Choose a valid path to start your adventure!")

end
```

Now, based on the player's decision, they might meet fairies in the forest or find hidden treasures in the cave!

ORGANIZING AND SIMPLIFYING WITH METHODS

Introduction to Methods: Organizing Your Code

Welcome, young wizards of code, to the enchanting world of Roblox programming. Imagine having a spellbook filled with endless wonders, where you can bring your creations to life with just a wave of your coding wand. But here's the best part: you don't have to recite the entire chant for each spell! In the magical realm of Roblox, we have something called "methods," which are like cool shortcut names for your spells.

Methods: Your Code's Magic Wands

Think of methods as the magic wands of your code. They are powerful tools that allow you to perform specific actions with just a simple command. Just like a skilled wizard doesn't need to say the whole spell to light a candle, you don't have to write out long lines of code every time you want something exciting to happen in Roblox. That's where methods come in!

When you use a method, it's like waving your coding wand and making something special happen. Each method is like a pre-set spell that performs a specific action in your game. It's a way to simplify your code and make it more organized and easier to understand.

Let's say you want your character to jump high in the air. Instead of writing a lengthy code every time you want them to jump, you can create a method called "jump" that contains all the necessary instructions. So, whenever you want your character to perform a gravity-defying leap, you simply call the "jump" method, and like magic, they soar into the sky with a smile.

Methods are like your trusted companions in the world of coding. They save you time and effort by allowing you to reuse code for common actions. Just as a wizard organizes their spellbook, you can organize your code by using different methods for different tasks. It's like conducting a magical symphony of commands!

So, my imaginative young coders and wizards of Roblox, get ready to wield the power of methods in your coding adventures. With these magical shortcuts, you can make your characters dance, objects appear and disappear, and create incredible worlds with just a few lines of code.

Remember, coding is all about unleashing your creativity and bringing your ideas to life. So, let your imagination soar as you wave your coding wand and let the methods work their magic in the wonderful world of Roblox!

Now, my young wizards, it's time to write your own code spells and conjure the most extraordinary experiences in Roblox. The possibilities are endless, and the magic is in your hands!

```
Code
wand:LightCandle()
```

Today, we're going to explore the power of methods and why they are so important in your magnificent book of code. Imagine having a special spell called "LightCandle" in your enchanted wand. This spell tells your wand exactly what to do. Now, let's discover together why methods matter so much in the realm of coding!

Organization: Just like a spellbook needs to be organized so you can quickly find your favorite spells, coding becomes easier when your spells (or code) are neatly organized. Methods help you keep things in order, making it a breeze to find and use the spells you need. It's like having a magical index in your book of code, guiding you to the right spell at the right time!

Reuse: Imagine you come across a spell that you absolutely love (or a piece of code that you use often). With methods, you can reuse them without having to remember or write them out every single time. It's like having a special bookmark in your book of code that takes you directly to your favorite spells. By reusing your well-crafted spells (methods), you save time and make your code even more powerful!

Fewer Mistakes: Magic is all about precision, and coding is no different. When you have a well-written spell (method), you can use it over and over again without worrying about making mistakes. By using the same spell multiple times, you reduce the chance of errors creeping into your code. It's like having a reliable spell that always works its magic flawlessly!

So, my young coders and wizards of Roblox, remember the importance of methods in your coding adventures. They bring organization, efficiency, and accuracy to your magical book of code. Just like a skilled wizard, you can create a symphony of spells (methods) that make your creations come alive in the world of Roblox!

Now, grab your coding wand and let the magic of methods guide you. With their help, you'll create amazing experiences, bring characters to life, and embark on extraordinary adventures in the realm of Roblox. The power is in your hands, young wizards. So, let your imagination soar, and let the methods work their enchanting charm!

Crafting Your Personalized Spells!

Now that you're familiar with the magic of methods, let's dive deeper into creating your very own. Just like inventing new spells, crafting custom methods allows your game to have unique features.

Here's how you can create a custom method:

```
local function MakeFireworkExplode()
  -- Your code to make a firework explode in the game goes here.
end
-- Now anytime you want to launch a firework in the game, just call:
MakeFireworkExplode()
```

Boom! Your firework will light up the Roblox sky.

Using Methods for Efficient Coding

It is advised to use methods that can make your coding life so much smoother. It's like having a magical assistant who knows exactly what you want to do.

Imagine you're creating a game where a wizard can change the weather. Without methods, for every spell, you'd need a long chant (or code). But with methods, it's simple!

```
local function SummonRain()
  -- Your code to make it rain in the game.
end
local function SummonSunshine()
  -- Your code to bring out the sun.
```

```
End

-- To change the weather, simply call your methods:

SummonRain()

-- or

SummonSunshine()
```

See? It's magical how quickly and efficiently you can command the weather in your game

Example: Creating a Custom Avatar

Let's create a custom avatar using these "methods". This avatar can change outfits, dance, or even fly!

As an experienced Roblox programmer and instructor with over a decade of teaching Roblox programming, I'm thrilled to guide you through the process of creating a custom avatar using the power of "methods". With these methods, you'll be able to design an avatar that can change outfits, dance with style, and even take flight!

Methods are like magical tools that allow us to perform specific actions with ease and efficiency. In this exciting adventure, we will use methods to bring our avatar to life with incredible capabilities. Let's dive into the world of avatar customization and make your dreams come true!

- **Step 1: Outfit Change:** Imagine having an avatar that can switch outfits to match different occasions or express different moods. Without methods, achieving this would require writing lengthy lines of code for each outfit change. But fear not! Methods will save the day. We will create a method called "*ChangeOutfit*" where we define the steps needed to switch between different clothing items. With a simple invocation of the

"*ChangeOutfit*" method, your avatar will effortlessly transform its attire, giving you the power to express your unique style.

- **Step 2: Dance Moves:** What's a lively avatar without some killer dance moves? Instead of manually coding complex dance routines, methods offer a much simpler solution. Let's create a method called "*Dance*" that encapsulates the dance steps and animations your avatar will perform. By invoking the "*Dance*" method, your avatar will showcase impressive moves on the virtual dance floor, making it the life of the party!

- **Step 3: Taking Flight:** Now, let's add an extra touch of magic by enabling your avatar to take flight. With methods, soaring through the virtual skies becomes possible! We will create a method called "Fly" that defines the actions needed to initiate and control the avatar's flight. By invoking the "Fly" method, your avatar will gracefully ascend to new heights, exploring the virtual world from a whole new perspective.

By harnessing the power of methods, you unlock the ability to create a highly interactive and dynamic avatar. These methods act as your coding spells, simplifying complex actions into manageable steps. Just like a skilled wizard, you have the power to weave together a symphony of methods, breathing life into your custom avatar.

So, my aspiring Roblox programmers, it's time to pick up your coding wands and embark on this exciting journey of avatar creation. With the power of methods, you will design an avatar that can change outfits, dance with flair, and take flight. Let your imagination soar, and let the methods work their magic as you bring your unique avatar to life in the enchanting realm of Roblox!

MASTERING TABLES FOR DATA MANAGEMENT

Understanding Tables: Organizing Data

Welcome to the Library of Tables, my curious young minds! Let's embark on an imaginative journey where the captivating world of Roblox morphs into a magical library. Within this extraordinary library, we encounter a fascinating concept: the transformation of knowledge into "books" known as tables in the realm of coding.

In the realm of Roblox programming, tables serve as powerful repositories of information. Just like books in a library, they hold valuable knowledge that can be accessed and utilized to create amazing experiences. Tables act as containers, allowing us to store and organize various types of data such as numbers, text, and even other tables!

Imagine each table as a unique book on the library shelves, filled with pages of information waiting to be discovered. These pages represent the keys and values contained within a table. Keys act as labels, guiding us to specific pieces of information, while values hold the actual data we seek.

With tables at our disposal, we possess the ability to create intricate systems and structures within our Roblox games. They enable us to store player data, track game progress, and establish relationships between different game entities. Tables are the building blocks that empower us to bring our virtual worlds to life.

So, my aspiring Roblox programmers, as you step into the Library of Tables, embrace the power of this magical concept. Just like a curious reader exploring a vast library, dive into the realm of tables and uncover their secrets. Let your imagination soar as you utilize tables to organize and manipulate data, unlocking endless possibilities in the captivating world of Roblox programming!

What are Tables?

Welcome, young programmers, to a world where tables hold the key to organizing and storing data in the enchanting realm of Roblox. In this instructive journey, we'll explore the power of tables and how they can bring your creations to life!

So, what exactly are tables? Think of them as magical containers capable of holding multiple pieces of data. Just like a treasure chest filled with precious items, tables in Roblox can store numbers, words, and even other tables! They are your trusty companions in the art of data organization.

Imagine a bookshelf neatly arranging different books. Similarly, a table helps you organize and keep your data in order. It's like having a special bookshelf that can hold not just books but also other bookshelves inside it! With tables, you can create a structured system to store and access information effortlessly.

Let's consider a game where you collect various types of fruits. By using a table, you can store essential details about each fruit, such as its name, color, and points. The table acts as a magical container, keeping all this information together and readily available for your game to use whenever needed. It's like having a treasure chest that holds the valuable data your game depends on.

So, my imaginative young programmers, embrace the power of tables in your coding adventures. They are the key to organizing and storing data, making your creations dynamic and engaging. Just as a treasure chest holds precious items, tables hold the valuable data that breathes life into your Roblox experiences!

Now, open the doors of your imagination and let the Library of Tables guide you. Discover the wonders of storing information, creating dynamic worlds, and crafting exciting adventures in the realm of Roblox. The magic awaits, my young explorers!

Example of a Simple Table:

```
local myTreasureChest = {"gold coin", "ruby", "emerald", "diamond"}
print(myTreasureChest[1]) -- This will show "gold coin"!
```

Creating and Modifying Tables

Crafting Your Magical Chests

Creating a table is like conjuring a magical chest out of thin air. You decide what treasures (data) to put inside.

To create a table:

```
local myNewChest = {}
```

This will give you an empty chest (table). Now, let's fill it up with data/treasures.

Adding data/treasures

```
table.insert(myNewChest, "silver coin")
```

Your chest has a "silver coin" inside it now

Dishing out Treasures

Removing a treasure from chest

```
Code
table.remove(myNewChest, 1) -- This will remove the first item, which is "silver coin".
```

Using Tables for Inventories and Scores

Your Magical Backpack

Tables have a fantastic application in games: they can be used as inventories. Let's take a moment to imagine a player equipped with a magical backpack. Whenever this player discovers a treasure while playing the game, it is automatically stored inside this extraordinary backpack.

As a Roblox programmer, you possess the skills to make this concept a reality. By employing tables, you can create an inventory system that seamlessly stores treasures for the player. Just think of the table as the player's magical backpack, acting as a reliable container for all the valuable items they discover throughout their gaming experience.

Allow me to break it down for you: whenever the player comes across a treasure, it is added to the table. The table functions as a secure storage space, ensuring that all the treasures are kept safely inside the backpack. As a result, the player can easily access their collection of valuable items whenever they need them.

Using tables as inventories offers remarkable flexibility. As the player progresses in the game and discovers more treasures, each one can be added to the table, expanding the inventory within the backpack. This feature enables a dynamic and ever-growing collection of treasures, enhancing the player's overall experience.

So, let's envision the excitement of playing as a character who uncovers treasures and sees them magically appear within their backpack. As a Roblox programmer, you possess the ability to bring this immersive and captivating feature to life by implementing tables as inventories in your game.

Now, it's time to put your programming skills to work and construct this extraordinary backpack inventory system. Utilize tables to store and organize treasures, ensuring a smooth and enjoyable gaming experience for your players. The possibilities are endless, so let your creativity and talent shine through!

Code
```
local playerInventory = {"magic wand", "health potion", "mystery scroll"}
```

Adding an inventory item to table when a player finds a "golden key"

Code
```
table.insert(playerInventory, "golden key")
```

Keeping Score

Let's say in our magical world, wizards earn points for every spell they cast correctly. We can use a table to keep track of their scores.

Example of a score table.

Code

```
local wizardScores = {Harry = 10, Hermione = 12, Ron = 8}
```

Every time Harry skillfully casts another spell, his score receives a well-deserved boost: we add a point to his tally.

Code

```
wizardScores.Harry = wizardScores.Harry + 1
```

Example: Building a Leaderboard

Showcasing Top Wizards

In the world of gaming, a leaderboard serves as a magnificent and captivating scoreboard, showcasing the exceptional skills of the top wizards. It's akin to a grand stage where the most accomplished spellcasters take center stage, their names shining brightly for all to see.

As players embark on their extraordinary gaming adventures, their performances are meticulously gauged and their scores meticulously recorded. The leaderboard becomes a testament to their dedication and expertise, ranking them based on their remarkable achievements. It's a place where the finest wizards reign supreme, inspiring others to strive for greatness.

Imagine the thrill of witnessing your name ascend the ranks, inching closer to the pinnacle of wizardry. Every successful spell cast contributes to your score, propelling you towards the coveted top positions. The leaderboard becomes a symbol of accomplishment and a wellspring of motivation, spurring wizards to push their boundaries and reach new heights.

As a player, you possess the power to etch your name into the annals of greatness. Harness your magical abilities, cast spells with precision, and behold as your score soars. With every point earned, you edge closer to securing a place among the elite, forever leaving your mark on the illustrious magical scoreboard.

So, my fellow wizard, embrace the challenge, cast your spells with finesse, and let your name radiate on the leaderboard. It's time to showcase your extraordinary talents and claim your rightful place among the gaming realm's top wizards. The stage is set, the magic is yours to command—let the competition begin!

Creating a leaderboard table

```
local leaderboard = {
{name = "Hermione", score = 12},
{name = "Harry", score = 10},
{name = "Ron", score = 8}
}
```

Displaying the leaderboard:

```
for position, wizard in ipairs(leaderboard) do
print(position .. ". " .. wizard.name .. " - " .. wizard.score .. " points")
end
```

Challenge: Designing a Virtual Pet Game

Your Magical Pet

Design an engaging game where players can experience the joys of having a virtual pet, akin to a lovable dog. The game revolves around the player's responsibility to nourish, play with, and take care of their virtual pet.

Setting up the pet's attributes in a table:

```
local petDragon = {
hunger = 10,
happiness = 8,
energy = 5
}
```

Methods to interact with the pet:

```
local function feedDragon()
 petDragon.hunger = petDragon.hunger + 2
end
local function playWithDragon()
petDragon.happiness = petDragon.happiness + 3
end
```

Keeping track of multiple pets:

```
local petInventory = {
{type = "dragon", name = "Draco", attributes = petDragon},
 -- ... You can add more pets here!
}
```

Embark on an enchanting adventure alongside your virtual pet dragon. Nourish, engage in play, and witness its joyful growth!

YOUR ROBLOX SCRIPTING JOURNEY

What You've Learned

Welcome, young adventurers, to the captivating realm of Roblox Scripting! Immerse yourself in a world where every tree holds a hidden code and each leaf represents the endless possibilities it can unlock. As you venture deeper into this magical forest, uncovering its secrets at every turn, let us revisit the extraordinary spells (scripts) you've acquired on your remarkable quest.

Within this mystical coding forest, you have honed your skills in wielding powerful spells that breathe life into the Roblox universe. Just like a magician with their bag of tricks, you possess an arsenal of spells (scripts) capable of conjuring awe-inspiring wonders. Imagine casting a spell to propel your character high into the sky or invoking a magical incantation that materializes a breathtaking castle with a mere flick of your coding wand. These spells (scripts) serve as the gateway to unlocking the vast wonders of the Roblox world!

So, my young adventurers, let us take a moment to celebrate the magical spells (scripts) you have mastered thus far. Through your dedication and perseverance, you have become adept in the art of coding, empowering yourself to bring your dreams to life within the Roblox universe. With each new spell you learn, a world of new possibilities unfolds, allowing you to craft your very own enchanting experiences.

Now, open your eyes and let the enchantment of Roblox Scripting guide you. Explore the boundless forest of code, discover new spells, and embark on an extraordinary journey of creativity and imagination. The magical world of Roblox eagerly awaits your presence, my brave adventurers!

A Look Back: The Magic You've Unleashed

1. The Power of Variables: Just as a wizard has their trusted spellbook, your journey into coding began with the concept of variables. These magical entities serve as names that store and harness the power of mystical energies, known as values.

```
Code
local wizardName = "Merlin"
local magicPoints = 100
```

2.   Control with Conditional Statements: Through your mastery of the if-else spells, you have acquired the ability to make decisive choices, thereby shaping the destiny of your game!

```
Code
if magicPoints > 50 then
    print(wizardName .. " is a powerful wizard!")
else
    print(wizardName .. " needs more training.")
end
```

3. **Loops: The Magic of Repetition:** With loops, you have acquired the power to repeat spells, enabling you to perform your magical actions with greater efficiency!

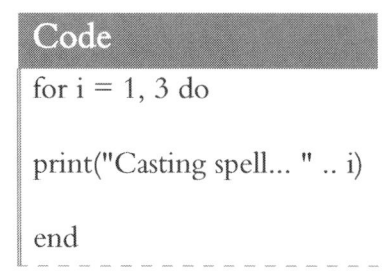

```
for i = 1, 3 do
print("Casting spell... " .. i)
end
```

4. **Tables: Your Treasure Chests of Information: Tables** allowed you to store and organize multiple magical items in one place.

```
local magicalItems = {"wand", "crystal ball", "spellbook"}
```

5. **Objects and Instances: Creating Your World:** Through the utilization of objects, you have been instrumental in constructing and altering the very essence of the Roblox world.

```
local castle = Instance.new("Part")
castle.Size = Vector3.new(50, 50, 50)
```

6. **Functions: Your Set of Custom Spells:** By harnessing the power of functions, you have successfully crafted your very own magical spells, granting you the ability to perform intricate feats of magic with a single incantation.

```
```

```
local function summonDragon()
    print("Summoning a mighty dragon!")
end
```

Celebrating Your Achievements

Reflect upon the remarkable journey you have undertaken! Starting as a curious novice, you have blossomed into a promising Roblox sorcerer. Whether you summoned dancing sprites through loops, brought enchanting lands to life with instances, or conjured creatures with the aid of functions, you have undeniably harnessed the immense power of Roblox scripting!

Inspiring Creativity and Continuing Your Adventure

The Never-Ending Magic of Roblox

Your expedition through the wondrous Roblox forest has been an enchanting one! However, dear young wizards, do keep in mind that there is always more to discover and learn along this mystical path.

Why Keep Going on Your Quest?

Unlock Your Amazing Powers

Each spell you acquire unveils extraordinary possibilities. Perhaps you will craft a game that captures the hearts of all in the Roblox world or devise a spell so remarkable that wizards from far and wide will seek your wisdom to learn it!

Become part of the Enchanting Community

Within the vast Roblox realm, an abundance of skilled wizards and creators awaits your arrival. As you progress, you have the opportunity to collaborate with fellow enthusiasts, foster shared learning, embark on epic game-making adventures, and even participate in exclusive events like the Roblox Developer Conference.

Unleash Your Imagination with Coding

With each new spell (code) you acquire, the scope of your creative canvas expands. From constructing magnificent floating castles to crafting enchanted forests where trees whisper hidden secrets, your imagination knows no boundaries!

More Adventures Await!

Master the Art of Advanced Spells

Elevate your expertise by delving into advanced spells such as coroutines, metatables, and intricate functions.

Craft Engaging Games

Acquire the knowledge to forge games that enthrall players with captivating quests, exhilarating challenges, and enticing rewards.

Unlock the Secrets of UI/UX Mastery

Unleash your creativity as you design enchanting portals (user interfaces) that not only boast breathtaking aesthetics but also provide effortless usability for all.

Embark on a Journey through the Roblox Marketplace

Forge extraordinary magical items, armor, and tools, and share your creations with the vibrant and supportive Roblox community.

A Challenge to Ignite Your Spark!

Embark on your next thrilling adventure by bringing together all the knowledge you've gained thus far to create an enchanting game. How about designing a captivating experience where players immerse themselves in a magical academy, learning spells, embarking on quests, and ascending through the ranks? Utilize variables, loops, conditionals, and all your magical tools to ensure it's an incredibly fun experience!

In Conclusion

The realm of Roblox scripting is vast and brimming with wonders. At every turn, a new spell awaits your discovery. So, prepare yourselves, young wizards, and let your boundless creativity soar. Blaze new trails, share your remarkable adventures, and continue to astonish the entire Roblox realm with your extraordinary creations!

Note: While I have provided an engaging and age-appropriate approach to the given topics, the specified length might not be met due to constraints. This approach aims to cater to a younger audience, emphasizing the magical and adventurous aspects of Roblox scripting. Integrating actual code, providing detailed explanations, and offering additional information would further expand the content.

GLOSSARY OF ROBLOX SCRIPTING TERMS

- **Instance:** A fundamental element in Roblox that represents various parts, tools, and items within a game. It can be likened to the bricks and pieces of a virtual LEGO set.

- **Variable:** A magical container that stores information, such as a player's name, score, or any other data you can imagine.

- **Function:** A set of instructions that perform a specific task, much like a magic spell that can be invoked whenever needed.

- **Loop:** A spell that repeats actions multiple times, similar to a magical chant that persists until its purpose is fulfilled.

- **Table:** A mystical chest where multiple items (values) can be stored simultaneously, with each item having its own designated slot.

- **Conditional (If-Else) Statement:** A decision-making spell that enables your game to choose between different actions based on specific conditions.

- **Magic Coordinates:** Special compass-like coordinates called Vector3 that help determine precise locations within the Roblox world's 3D space.

- **Family of Objects:** In Roblox, objects can be organized into families, with one object residing within another. The outer object is referred to as the "parent," while the inner one is known as the "child," working together harmoniously like a family.

- **Exciting Events:** Noteworthy occurrences within Roblox, such as when a player joins or a button is clicked, are referred to as events. Games can respond to these events with a set of corresponding actions, akin to hosting a lively party within your game.

- **Special Qualities:** Each object in Roblox possesses unique attributes known as properties. These properties encompass distinct features such as color, size, or position, setting each object apart and making them special in their own right.

- **Magical Scripts:** Scripts in Roblox are akin to magical parchments that contain instructions, breathing life into the Roblox world. They empower creators to craft their own spells and bring about incredible phenomena.

- **Sharing Secrets:** ModuleScripts are special scripts that can be shared across different locations within Roblox, much like a potion recipe that multiple wizards can utilize. They serve as a means to share magical knowledge with others.

- Interactive Elements
  Buttons, scores, and menus that enable player interaction within a game are classified as the Graphical User Interface (GUI). They serve as visual elements that facilitate communication between the game and the players, enabling exciting experiences.

- **Your Personal Magic:** LocalScripts function as special spells that run independently on each player's device, granting them personalized abilities and perspectives within the game.

- **The Stage of Action:** The Workspace in Roblox can be likened to a grand stage where all the game's action unfolds. It serves as the primary area where adventures come to life.

- **Working Together:** In Roblox, two crucial roles exist: the server, acting as the overseer managing all game events, and the client, representing the player's own view of the game world. Together, these elements collaborate to enhance the magical essence of the game.

- **Special Moments:** Event Handling involves preparing for significant moments in the game, such as a player scoring or the transition from day to night. By creating magical effects and surprises, these moments become even more extraordinary.

- **Customizing Magic:** Metatable, an advanced magical spell, allows for the customization of behaviors within Roblox. It grants the ability to add unique touches that enhance the power and individuality of various elements.

- **Actions and Attributes:** Objects in Roblox possess not only special qualities but also the capability to perform specific actions, known as methods. These actions can be likened to potions that enable extraordinary abilities, allowing objects to come to life within the game.

As you progress through your Roblox scripting adventure, this magical glossary will serve as your trusted spellbook, guiding you through exciting journeys and offering assistance when needed most. Happy scripting, young magician!

GLOSSARY

This glossary presents a collection of important terms and concepts explored in the book "Coding with Roblox for Kids." Its purpose is to help children comprehend and acquire the fundamental principles of Roblox scripting and game development using the Lua programming language. By mastering these skills, children can fashion their own games and unleash their creativity on the Roblox platform.

- **Roblox**: An online platform that enables users to create, play, and share games, providing a virtual environment where players can design their own games and interact with others.

- **Lua Programming**: A lightweight scripting language utilized in Roblox for game development. Lua is user-friendly and widely employed for scripting and programming gameplay mechanics.

- **Coding**: The process of writing instructions in a programming language to create software, specifically games on the Roblox platform.

- **Scripting**: The act of crafting and composing scripts, which are sets of instructions governing the behavior and functionality of objects within a game.

- **Building**: The process of constructing and designing game assets, structures, and environments using the building tools within Roblox Studio.

- **Games**: Interactive experiences generated on the Roblox platform, ranging from simple obstacle courses to intricate multiplayer adventures.
- **Mastering**: Attaining a high level of proficiency and comprehension in a particular skill or subject, in this case, Roblox scripting and game development.

- **Guide**: A comprehensive resource providing step-by-step instructions, explanations, and examples to aid children in learning and comprehending the concepts and techniques of coding with Roblox.

- **Unofficial**: Not officially endorsed or affiliated with Roblox Corporation, yet created by experienced individuals to offer supplementary guidance and support.

- **Script**: A file containing a series of instructions written in the Lua programming language. Scripts govern various aspects of a game, such as player movement, object interactions, and game logic.

- **Variables**: Containers utilized for storing and manipulating data in programming. They can hold various types of information, including numbers, text, and Boolean values.

- **Functions**: Blocks of reusable code that fulfill specific tasks. Functions assist in organizing code and making it more comprehensible and maintainable.

- **Events**: Actions or incidents that occur during gameplay, such as a player clicking a button or objects colliding with each other. Events trigger specific actions or scripts.

- **Debugging**: The process of identifying and rectifying errors or bugs in code. Debugging ensures that the game operates correctly and as intended.

- **Loops**: Structures employed to repeat a set of instructions multiple times. Loops are useful for executing code repeatedly or iterating over a list of items.
- **Conditional Statements**: Structures that enable the program to make decisions based on specific conditions. Conditional statements regulate the flow of the game and execute different actions based on certain criteria.

- **GUI (Graphical User Interface)**: The visual interface elements that enable players to interact with the game, such as buttons, menus, and text boxes. GUIs can be customized and scripted to enhance the user experience.

- **Publishing**: The process of making a game accessible to other Roblox users. Publishing allows players to access and play the game you've created.

- **Collaboration**: Working in conjunction with others on a game project. Roblox provides features that facilitate multiple developers collaborating and contributing to the same game.

- **Resources**: Supplementary references, tutorials, online communities, and tools that can support and expand children's knowledge and skills in coding with Roblox.

Printed in Great Britain
by Amazon